Bear Likes to Share

Therese Shea

NEiGHBORHOOD READERS

Rosen Classroom Books & Materials™

New York

"I like berries," said Bear.

"I like berries," said Deer.

"I like berries," said Fox.

"I like berries," said Rabbit.

"I like berries," said Bird.

"I like berries," said Mouse.

"We like berries!" they said.